Barefoot Luxury

MEXICAN RESORT LIVING

SANDRA ESPINET

Barefoot Luxury

MEXICAN RESORT LIVING

GIBBS SMITH
TO ENRICH AND INSPIRE HUMANKIND

To all of the helicopter flights and marshmallow dreams that have kept my creativity and inspiration alive.

CONTENTS

INTRODUCTION

I have been asked so many times what it is like to live and work as an American expat in the small and somewhat remote resort town of San Jose del Cabo, at the southern tip of Baja California del Sur, Mexico. My answer is honestly that because of my dual residency, much of my professional and social life still continues to revolve around Los Angeles. Yet the space and vistas and casual lifestyle of Baja help me refine my notion of a luxurious enclave away from the mass production and commonplace convenience of more popular vacation destinations. Part of my continuing fascination with marquee resort properties is the blend of remoteness and comfort, like the safari tent in Rajasthan, India, or a compartment on the Orient Express. By living so much of my life in my Baja "outpost," where imports must be carefully considered, I am better able to sift through design essentials and design overkill.

I can actually beta test with my own two feet the plushness of a custom rug carefully commissioned to cover a terrace on the edge of the earth. I live and travel back and forth between Cabo and Los Angeles, and this splitting of time enables me to feel and experience the calm Zen of living on a beautiful and dramatic beach in a casual Mexican fishing town while still getting my fix of urban attraction, art, and contemporary culture back in the States. It's the perfect arrangement for my mind to experience the yin of relaxation and the yang of activity. The allure of the faraway shore and the comforts of civilization. The barefoot and the luxurious.

I've always been infatuated with the storied luxury hotels of the world. I've thrilled to the exclusive ambiance and elegant discretion of jet-set destinations; the glamorous mystique

of the Aman Resorts or the Six Senses Hotels; how the fashionable bustle of the tony lobbies contrasts with the reverent hush of impossibly long hallways, all of it mingling with the ghosts of bygone movie stars, mistresses, and magnates. But I never imagined this sideline obsession would intersect with my actual interior design career, or allow me to use these rarefied milieus as aesthetic touchstones for the residential resort environments I would create along the dazzling coastlines of Mexico.

After graduating from the New England School of Design and then the Atlanta College of Art, I was hired as a junior hospitality designer by a succession of architecture and design firms, ultimately culminating with a position at the sublime Ocean Reef Club in North Key Largo, Florida. There I quickly became enthralled with the lifestyles of the senior designers, who traveled the world in order to absorb traditional and exotic design features and then translate them into unique experiences for the swelling ranks of the new affluent traveler. My design mentors knew how to distinguish between traditional and trendy and, even more, how to create impressive rooms with a sense of tasteful fantasy and plush comfort in equal measure. The hospitality industry is where I got my feet wet, so to speak. To this day, I have huge respect for

the interior designers, architects, purchasing agents and executives who work in the design of upscale hotels, resorts, restaurants, spas and other hospitality-oriented projects.

In order to remain fresh and current in the creation of my own trademark resort-inspired residential endeavors, I routinely patronize five-star luxury hotels and resorts the world over. Not just to enjoy the beauty and the spa-like amenities but also to keep up with my amazing peers in the hospitality field. Their passion for originality, perfection, and over-all excellence is a huge source of inspiration for me. I'm always amazed with the service, style, and design of hotels like the Rosewood

Mayakoba in Playa del Carmen, Mexico, or the Amanjiwo Hotel in Borobudur, Indonesia, or the Singhita in South Africa. I agree with my expanding clientele that one of the ultimate luxuries in life is to be able to live as if you were on a protracted holiday, in an amazing location, replete with a spectacularly comfortable and stylish interior. In short, I design residential retreats of sorts with all of the appointments, amenities, and considerations of a superb hotel. I try to replicate the quietly elegant, palpably informal perfection of these pampered yet uncluttered and unpretentious environments for my clients and my own personal life. This is the essence of what I call "barefoot luxury."

ESCAPE TO MEXICO

The meteoric rise of the Mexican resort as an elite destination for luxury, adventure, and relaxation is relatively recent, all things considered. Certainly since the nineteenth century, intrepid foreign visitors have braved arduous travel, bad roads, poor accommodations, murderous banditos, and parasite-riddled water to experience the violent beauty of Mexico's desert habitats, mountain ranges rising dramatically from steaming jungles, and unspoiled stretches of coastline. But after the Mexican revolution, the government of the new republic settled on promoting tourism as a primary strategy for achieving modernization. Mass development of infrastructure did, in fact, draw a new breed of tourist (less bushwhacker, more beachcomber) to the colonial cities, cultural festivals, and monumental Pre-Columbian architecture—the very heart of Mexican culture—in addition to the sparkling aqua seas and pillowy-soft sand. By the 1960s, the tourism industry was fully flourishing, as Americans and Canadians of varying back-

grounds and means flocked to well-protected resort destinations built from scratch to cater almost exclusively to Anglo tastes and high standards of convenience.

Mexican tourism officials may beg to differ and credit the country's surge in popularity to its natural beauty, a rugged wild coastline scalloped with hidden coves, and new national highways crisscrossing the country and connecting it to El Norte; but if you ask me, the resort revolution was really sparked by a tabloid-fueled movie star scandal. A quiet, sleepy little coastal village found itself thrust into the spotlight during the filming of Tennessee Williams's provocative *Night of the Iguana* in 1962. Paparazzi snapshots of Richard Burton and Elizabeth Taylor drinking local beer at al fresco bars and cavorting along pristine beaches were immediately devoured by an international public fascinated by the love life of the world's most famous woman. The Taylor-Burton affair turned Puerto Vallarta into a well-known tour-

ist destination. Burton himself purchased a nine-bedroom villa in town for Taylor as her thirty-second birthday present, and one for himself across the street. A customized bridge romantically linked the two residences together. Today, Casa Kimberly is a meticulously restored boutique hotel with Bulgari toiletries, private Jacuzzis, rainfall showers, and Taylor's own pink marble heart-shaped tub. You could say that Puerto Vallarta taught the world to pronounce the double L of an exotic Spanish-speaking outpost and set the pace and appetite for the type of elite resort playgrounds that sprung up seemingly overnight.

Here in the twenty-first century, a constellation of five-star beachfront retreats along the Pacific Ocean, the Sea of Cortez, and the Gulf of Mexico serve as self-contained worlds for the wealthiest and most discerning of vacation seekers. But real luxury these days is less about ostentation and entourage, and more about discretion and privacy. To

adapt to the evolved proclivities of the new breed of extreme wealth, the resort communities I work with in Mexico offer private residences within the exclusive enclave, as well as luxury furnishings and products that are specifically tailored to environmentally friendly and locally sustainable specifications for the eco-minded CEO and high-profile celebrity.

My design strategies amount to seductive provocations, gentle coercions, and exotic enchantments that integrate these new preferences for informality and a lighter footprint. The most successful pathway to these laid-back clearings situated in and around the increasingly seductive and luxurious Mexican resort society is through a blatant appeal to the senses—naturally plush tactile environments, an enveloping sense of spaciousness, and the quiet joy of walking through the world barefoot. Follow me as I take you on a tour of this elusive, yet aspirational, paradise. But first, please take your shoes off.

Two spectacular entrances make striking architectural statements and illustrate the rich artisanal carving tradition of Mexico. Cantera, a soft volcanic stone, has been used for centuries as a primary construction material in colonial Mexican cathedrals and haciendas. Patterns I created for a cantera border surrounding a mahogany front door were fabricated in Guadalajara by fifth-generation carvers. ABOVE: The design for the massive custom-carved cantera facade is an exaggerated Mexican baroque motif I borrowed from a church in San Miguel de Allende. The large Talavera pots come from Guanajuato.

For this cozy circular room, I wanted to collaborate with the view of the Sea of Cortez, not compete with it. A palette of creamy neutrals, accented with touches of teal, is not only easily approachable but gives the residents maximum appreciation of the coastal setting. The centerpiece of the room is a congregation of individual "root" tables, staggered in varying heights, that warm the space and lend a note of whimsy.

An open floor plan encompasses living and dining areas in a Mexican mountainside villa overlooking the Pacific Ocean. Natural elements evocative of the landscape keep the great room earthy and masculine, while walls of glass bring nature indoors. The vaulted ceiling is constructed of reclaimed beams; the customized dining table from a slab of maple has a sculptural bronze pedestal. I love to feel grounded with the wood and the bronze and then look up to see glimmering globes. Custom-made chandeliers from John Pomp Studios.

For the long-running balcony of a penthouse villa, I designed a custom-carved bifold screen to open across the entire length of the terrace. Furnishings include a vintage painted Moroccan table, chaise from Janus et Cie, and earthenware pots sourced from Asia and Mexico.

The cobblestone-lined streets of San Jose del Cabo's colorful arts district form the cultural heart of Baja Sur. The galleries themselves are exquisite examples of Mexican colonial architecture, housed in repurposed homes and shops well within walking distance of seaside piers, like this one in Playa del Carmen, which juts straight out into the beach break.

Custom light fixtures hang in the vaulted great room of a Cabo home, adding high-impact drama to the massive space. The white-on-white color scheme connects a series of sitting and dining areas, both inside and out, from a great room to a loggia to a terrace that leads straight to the beach. Strokes of red, blue and gold nod to the bold color tradition of Mexico.

A *palapa* shelters a dining area mere steps from a pool and the Pacific Ocean. A custom, polished travertine table, mesh chairs by Kettal, and a Jorge Marin sculpture complete the rocky beach vignette.

This homeowner's kitchen anchors a large, open plan great room, so it needs to look pretty more than it needs to function as the "muscle" for heavy-duty culinary work. That action takes place in a proper chef's kitchen behind the door on the right. But for light breakfasts and ad hoc snacking all day, this work station is perfect and discreet. The island mosaic is a custom design installed on-site by a local artisan; I sourced the tiles for the backsplash in Guanajuato.

RIGHT: This natural maple headboard was handcrafted by an artisan in upstate New York. The split design amplifies the live-edge rusticity of the bed and collaborates effortlessly with the reclaimed beams. Framed photography by Tomas Spangler of old doors in San Miguel de Allende flank the bed.

Architectural remnants and a carved wall distinguish these three guest bedrooms. The chest at the foot of the canopied bed is from San Miguel de Allende; the vintage wrought-iron light fixture is from Guadalajara. An extremely large Moroccan carpet grounds a pair of custom queen beds; a large *mestizo* portrait by David Villa Senor animates wall space. Reclaimed carved and mirrored panels are converted into art and pressed into service on either side of a custom-upholstered headboard.

In a sophisticated resort home office, a painting by famed Mexican muralist David Alfaro Siqueiros presides over a colonial Mexican desk, vintage tribal rug, and terra-cotta Mayan statue. Paneled leather walls and dark coffered ceilings keep the room moody and masculine. An antique Italian settee delivers a dash of haute charm.

LEFT: A game room with a bar and pool table is a great place to hang out when you don't feel like going out. The bar area features locally crafted leather stools and custom-made carved bar with iron railing. The carved wood ceiling with faux finish and a back-wall mosaic of broken mirror add visual interest. ABOVE: For a media room, I had three cross-sections of giant cypress trunks installed on the wall space above the capacious custom-made sofa. These pieces weigh a ton and required several men and special hardware to mount them. I stay away when this kind of work is happening! One of my rugs from Aga John anchors the space; I found the little bronze tables in New York.

RIGHT: This home office features standout local custom carving for the ceiling, bookcase, and reproduction eighteenth-century doors. An architectural remnant is used as a valence for window treatments. The French chairs are from Ebanista; Mestizo Indian portrait by David Villa Senor.

I believe guest rooms should have all the comforts of a luxury hotel as well as a cool, restful vibe. I recommend keeping them relatively uncluttered so that guests can personalize the space themselves. Here, a custom-upholstered headboard, acrylic bench, soft neutrals, ample pillows, and a Baja landscape painting by local artist Rafael Chavez constellate to create a soothing and sumptuous sanctuary.

LEFT: A mirror by renowned Mexican artist Jesus Guerrero Santos overlooks a vanity hand carved out of one piece of Crema Marfil Marble from Spain. ABOVE: I converted a console into a vanity and outfitted it with a low-profile vessel sink in onyx. I found the tiles in Guanajuato and had them custom colored in a neutral light fawn. The wood mirror is custom made and then silvered.

The headboard, nightstands, and chaise were all custom crafted from reclaimed railroad ties. I left the wood for the headboard raw to echo the rusticity of the ceiling beams and upholstered it with cowhide. The vintage handmade Moroccan rug is from Woven Accents; chair and ottoman by Jens Risom.

I designed this transitional beach bedroom in shades of sand and blue. A pair of local abstract paintings worked beautifully with the color scheme. For a powder room, I found a silver mirror handcrafted by a local artisan and converted a Talavera bowl into a vessel sink. The vanity is a custom-made table outfitted with a slab of travertine. A vintage Moroccan lamp can be seen reflected in the mirror.

Inspired by a fire pit with a fountain feature
I had seen in China, I created this unique
"fire fountain" for a courtyard living area
in a Mexican villa. Besides the idea of
combining two powerful forces—fire
and water—in one arresting focal point,
my design for the space also juxtaposes
modern and traditional elements. The
back wall fountain is composed of local
Talavera tile and carved cantera spouts,
traditional Mexican building components
that work well with old stone masonry and
classic wrought iron. But the hand-chiseled
cantera fire pit with the waterfall feature
brings the composition into the modern
realm. Green and red pillows fashioned
from vintage textiles adorn contemporary
Janus et Cie chairs. The massive terra-cotta
pot is from San Miguel de Allende.

Under a Banksy painting I sit, my bare feet resting upon reclaimed wood from France, beautifully laid out in a graphic chevron pattern. I love bedrooms, and this one opens up to a charming terrace. I designed a four-poster bed swagged with sheer drapery. Everywhere else, the fabric is Fortuny. Architectural remnants are converted into valences, and even curtain rods. The chaise by Donghia is upholstered in a Tibetan silk wool.

LEFT: Colorful paper lanterns and *papel picado* banners crisscross a cobblestone street in downtown San Jose Del Cabo. ABOVE: Another restful bedroom, with wall art by an artist from San Miguel de Allende who paints bougainvillea petals.

A balance of luxe furnishings and natural touches defines this living room. The design is an evocation of ocean breezes and the rugged wild coastline—simple and earthy, effortless and captivating.

THE REINVENTED RETREAT

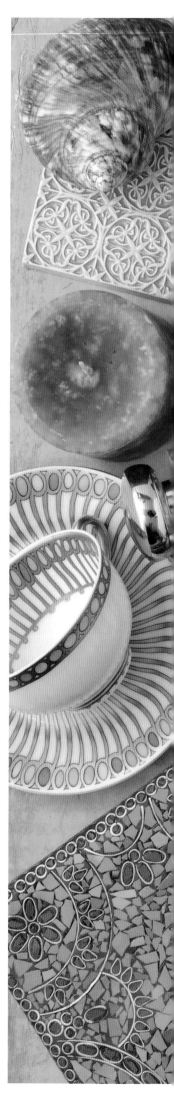

Sometimes clients will describe a design scheme they'd like for a new home or the renovation of an old one by blurting out, "What we really want is something like the public rooms and private suites at the Mauna Kea, or the outdoor showers at the Six Senses Vietnam, or the pool at the Agra Oberoi. And, of course, I know exactly what they mean: the seamlessly elegant blend of spacious and serenely textured privacy that is the hallmark of celebrated upscale resorts. My shorthand reference for this aesthetic is "barefoot luxury."

For most of the twentieth century, ensemble activities and seasonal fun such as meals, parties and recreational excursions were an expected component of resort life, and vacationing strangers joined in with a spirit of camaraderie. But over time, resorts began to evolve the getaway experience towards accommodations with more flexibility, more

options for privacy, and more personal tailoring. Most marquee resorts these days provide semi-adjacent bungalows complete with kitchens, private pools, and maybe even dedicated staff; but these enclaves, although separate from the main stage, still feel like satellites of the hallways, lobbies, bellhops, and the crowded concierge desks of the flagship building and still vibrate with the hum and bustle of the resort itself. And that's not for everyone.

At some point in the late '60s and early '70s along the west coast of Mexico, and earlier in the Caribbean, a wave of separate residential properties began to spring up near the established beachheads of grand resorts, which were located to take advantage of the natural magic of the most prime coastline beauty. I've seen scores of these first-generation vacation homes and villas; the early incarnations were

pretty uninspired, maybe even banal. They were uncertain of their form or function and lifted a majority of aesthetic features from the efficiencies of single-family homes found everywhere. Eventually, and fortuitously for me, a new trend began to emerge that realized the luxurious potential of these private villas in the grand manner of first-class resorts: expanses of plate glass, open plan room geometries, and rarified exotic decor. By maximizing the combination of resort elegance and otherworldly comfort, along with the privacy and seclusion of the personal residence simply transferred to a shimmering strand of beach, the reinvented retreat is now a hybrid of top-drawer hospitality perks and barefoot ease. It's also my design sweet spot.

Collaborating with architects before the construction phase allows me to layer texture in travertine, tile, and sisal along spacious floors and hallways; install panels of carved wood, reclaimed timber, or sliced stone; or arrange rooms on offset angles to overlook breathtaking poolscapes through unbroken walls of glass or recessed sliding doors. The furnishings themselves can speak to the seductive dialogue between indoor and outdoor, between arrival and departure, between lazy and lively. In spaces such as these, and with clients so inclined, I can really hit the bull's-eye of this barefoot luxury idiom, providing an escape from the everyday, a luxurious sanctuary from the laborious journey, a stunningly sumptuous and discreet playground. These commissions are certainly retreats, but they are scaled and sourced to replicate the reassuring effects of really excellent resorts, the types of rooms that encourage both action and relaxation—recommending neither, yet creating a sense of possibility for both. *Vamonos!*

Masterworks of artisanal tradition, these sinuously carved Mexican panels don't just separate a hallway from the living area; they bring high drama to a glamorous Cabo beach home. Curved sofa by Donghia; custom silk wool rug hand loomed in Nepal; rock marble and iron-base tables handcrafted locally.

Sometimes the little details can have a surprising impact on a vignette that might otherwise be overlooked. I had this quartet of iron chairs (with the divinely unexpected backs) replicated from a 1940s original I had stumbled upon in Paris. Brass nailhead trim adds classic elegance to a customized lacquered-linen game table. Above: Modern Italian wall sconces contrast whimsically with a rustic floating wood console by Mimi London.

Neutrals don't have to feel cold and minimal. This sand-hued bedroom designed for a couple of tall, basketball-playing teen boys delivers a look of relaxed warmth and inviting comfort. Vintage storage trunks are from India; I found the antique *vaquero* hats in a Mexico City antique shop; the vintage inlaid bone-and-wood mirror is from Morocco.

Colorful bougainvillea grows naturally wild all over Mexico. For the outdoor shower space of a private enclosed patio overlooking the ocean, I created the terra-cotta tile design and customized the colors to complement the earthy hues that dominate the home's interior.

Behind the upholstered bed, three slabs of translucent bookmarked marble create an intricate and luxurious palette of colors when backlit at night. Facing the (unseen) indoor master bedroom pool, sumptuously oversized chairs from Link Outdoor are upholstered in an edgy outdoor fabric. Swivel daybed on covered terrace by Dedon. Floors are traditional Mexican river rock.

Two hand-hammered silver doors from Oaxaca have been converted into headboards. Aʙᴏᴠᴇ: rustic meets chic when the vintage bed and simple antique Mexican chest mix it up with modern ottoman and chair from Ralph Pucci in a seamless blend of classic and contemporary. Rɪɢʜᴛ: A teal glass Venetian lamp from Donghia and custom-colored linen by Anali look sleek, cultured, and elegant against the elaborately etched silver headboard.

Thoroughly modern Mexico.
A crisp, chic bar area connects
with the living room via a
palette of cool, clean blues
and whites. Ralph Pucci
chairs. Vintage sunburst
chandelier from Venice, Italy.
Metallic wave photograph
by Peter Lick. Cow fur
rug from Kyle Bunting.

Infused with a medley of patterns in teal, this room's edited palette makes it a soothing sanctuary. A sand dollar mirror adds a beachy flourish. On the terrace, a hanging daybed from Dedon supplies the perfect perch for ocean gazing.

A guest room with a regal vibe. The dramatic bed was custom made in San Miguel de Allende. The antique Spanish trunk and Virgin of Guadalupe figure deliver Latin American flair, while the fearless use of patterns adds visual interest and exotic energy. Shades of blue keep the room unified.

A completely private master bath with an indoor/outdoor shower featuring two side wall shower heads and a ceiling-mounted rain shower head. I designed the tile floor to resemble a rug. The lithe iron table is from Minton Spidel; vintage Moroccan tables and a daybed grace the terrace.

The exquisite shape of this Indonesian chandelier from Irony in Los Angeles would make the fixture an instant focal point in any room. Here, in a master bath, it presides over a capacious travertine bathtub. Right: I carved a sweet, simple guest room out of a small space by extending the headboard all the way across the ceiling. The high gloss adds an unexpected stroke of contemporary flair.

As requested by my client, everything in her beachfront master bedroom is dressed with the enduring tones of blue and white, further reiterating the presence of sea and sand just beyond her window. RIGHT: A vanity area is totally mirrored. Slender glass candleholders and cream accessories keep the room more feminine, less exotic.

My client fell in love with this luscious, almost-Orientalist floral fabric; so we designed her master bedroom around it. An antique Indian chest inlaid with iridescent mother-of-pearl, an old Indian fireplace screen upholstered and converted into a headboard, a teal-and-cream urn from Morocco, and other found treasures create a romantic yet playful environment for the most personal room in the house.

LEFT: The warm woods and cool blue palette of this bedroom pay tribute to the stark desert aspect of the Baja Peninsula. A very old door sourced in San Miguel de Allende has been pressed into headboard service. An even older Indian chest contributes to the subtle rustic textures. ABOVE: A dynamic bedroom interior mixes contemporary pieces and reflective surfaces for a modern vibe.

A large penthouse villa overlooks the Pacific Ocean. While this cozy open floor plan is grounded in a traditional, tailored style, the mix of finishes and textures creates visual interest. The sand and stone palette gives the space a natural, relaxed feeling. Furniture by Mimi London. Light fixtures, indoors and out, custom made in Cabo.

A guard station at Playa Palmilla, an extremely popular white sand beach on a crescent-shaped cove. The calm waters make it perfect for diving, snorkeling, and swimming.

CALM, COOLTH, AND COLLECTED

I've always made excellent use of regional neutrals—sun-bleached woods and blanched stone; natural linens and earthy sisals—as well as the most striking spot on the color wheel: the red zone. The full range of *rojo* includes everything from the fevered scarlet tones of hibiscus to the peachy pinks of bougainvillea and the burnt clays of hard-baked floor pavers. Serapes, dripware, and leather goods "made in Mexico" have exhausted every shade of red from shrimp to carmine, and so have I! I love fuchsias and magentas, verging into jaspers and cinnabars, and merging into persimmons and corals like nobody's business.

But after a few seasons in the self-perpetuating hot seat, so to speak, I decided to slow down the collective pulse rate of my new designs and take a long, deep breath. I was in need of a counterpoint. These days I'm completely captivated by the multitude of blue hues swelling in the depths off the Baja coastline. I love splashes of cobalt, turquoise and lapis lazuli, and the look of crisp teal pillows on a long-lined sofa. I'm intrigued by how exquisitely sky blue and robin's egg work for upholstered bed frames and bedding textiles.

The tonal variations on what is essentially the dark side of the color wheel calm the mind, soothe the soul, and paradoxically invigorate the spirit. I love to use local artisanal fabrics in every blue and blue-green out there—from sea foam to cerulean and all the indigo-inspired allies. I like jewel-like blue tiles on floors, stairways, fountains, and backsplashes. Who doesn't appreciate the relief from the ochres and sands of the desert when it encounters an oasis of tourmaline glass or celadon mosaic? Not only do quieter shades invite us to rest the retina, they actually flatter everyone and everything else in the room. Blue is the color of contemplation, but the aquamarine iridescence of the coastline at dusk inspires a flight

of fantasy like no other. Throw in the soothing thunder of crashing waves and you're definitely not in Kansas anymore.

All the blues and greens I use in my interiors are gorgeous in and of themselves, but they function best as sly accomplices to the real showstopping inspirations of my Mexican and Central American designs: the Sea of Cortez and the Pacific Ocean. Talk about an excellent wingman; the endless vistas over placid or churning seas are unmatchable. So I make every effort to incorporate them into my interior work: I remove walls, expand windows, elevate beds and even entire rooms for ultimate access to an ocean view.

Sapphire blue pillow fabrics and bean green glazed patio pottery, aqua chaise lounges, and even pool table felting and festive glassware are especially dazzling when close to the sea. It's all a crescendo of coolth, an invitation to rest and gaze, and then head out for a swim or grab a board and paddle out past the breakers.

Don't get me wrong, I still love the tangerines and mangos that express the hot beat of the tropics and the burning heat of the desert. But I must admit that lately I prefer that family of color that doesn't assault the newly arrived guest like a bear hug of toreador red. Ocean tones lure us to them with the peaceful promise of refreshment and escape. Like bare feet stepping into the surf, the use of blue in my work conveys a vibe of cool stimulation. The tranquility of the seashore carried by flowing breezes into wide-open windows envelops whomever is present in a calm and restorative pause. But it's all just pre-production. Sometimes you want to throw on a fiery red dress, knock back a few shots of Oaxacan mezcal, and hit the dance floor with a bronzed windsurfer or scratch golfer. Go for it. You're already well rested.

At a magnificent resort home on the Pacific, the pool area is lined by aluminum chaise longues topped with terry cloth–covered cushions from McKinnon and Harris. Cheery hand-painted umbrellas further enliven the scene. The built-in banquette with vibrant accent pillows extends the home's color theme right down to the surf.

In guest bedrooms I love to integrate furnishings and fixtures crafted entirely by hand using primitive practices. A reclaimed beam delivers a rough-hewn sensibility, while a wrought iron headboard conveys the spirit of Mexico in one glance. Aga John rugs; fabric by Manuel Canovas.

A custom island topped with a slab of quartzite serves as an impromptu dining area in a contemporary kitchen with traditional Cabo flourishes. Above the island, a hammered iron light fixture from Kneedler Fauchere drops from a *bóveda* ceiling constructed with reclaimed old bricks. Hand-baked tiles from Country Floors create the backsplash. Chairs by A. Rudin.

LEFT: A summer palette of blue and white belongs inside the home just as much as outside. This Cabo kitchen is kept casual and beachy with beadboard cupboards, a simple tile design, and local pottery. ABOVE: Modern shapes and finishes mingle with traditional Mexican details in this open floor living environment.

Baja California Sur is a state of mind. Carefree, colorful, and relaxed, it can be summoned with an outdoor fire pit, umbrella fabric, and playful wicker furniture. Red is not an accent color I generally use, but when the mood strikes, olé! Synthetic wicker chairs custom made in Indonesia.

Delightful al fresco vignettes celebrate the indoor/outdoor lifestyle of Baja and seem to appear around every turn. RIGHT: Enveloped by palms and tropical flora, this lovely spot is a perfect private hideaway away from the crowd, beckoning you to rest and relax. Outdoor woven daybed by Dedon. Vietnamese ceramic pot.

This guest room blends warm wood, gentle curves, and vivid color for a clean, traditional look that works all year round. Custom-made rug; large painted pot from Guanajuato.

I like to build a space around high-impact statements, such as this eye-catching custom-designed cantera stone fireplace. The colorful blue urns were sourced in Guanajuato. Lounge chairs from Wicker Works; stone table from Formations.

My client requested a bedroom that felt luxurious and casual at the same time. The four-poster bed custom-made in Guadalajara is grand, but with vividly patterned textiles it imparts a look of relaxed refinement. The rich rose hue of the headboard and bedding is picked up in the carpet. I dressed up the room with traditional Spanish Colonial accessories and landscape paintings.

This mostly neutral living room is broken up with dark ceiling beams and splashes of persimmon. For go-barefoot casual warmth, a custom rug is layered over smooth travertine. The iron and stone glass-topped coffee table is custom. Beach painting by local artist Dennis Wentworth Porter.

An abstract painting is the perfect accomplice for a pair of vintage chairs and a modern occasional table in an otherwise neglected hallway. Chairs and table from Circa, Los Angeles..

Every Thursday during high season, San Jose del Cabo closes down a few streets in the Gallery District for the weekly Art Walk. Art lovers and tourists stroll through the galleries sipping wine and dine at restaurants long into the night.

To enhance the tropical style of this home, I covered the plump sofas and chairs in an off-white fabric to keep the look light, simple, and casual. The whitewashed space is energized with a few carefully selected pieces, including a colorful painting by a local Mexican artist.

For these Cabo guest rooms, I massed colors of pink, orange, fuchsia, and marigold to eye-popping effect. Bright and beautiful, fun and fresh, they stand in colorful contrast to the rest of the earth-hued home. Custom-made jute rug; fabrics by Manuel Canovas.

Modern rustic comfort meets traditional Mexico in this luxuriously laid-back resort living room. An old beam remnant converted into a valence contains an electrically operated wall-sized reed window treatment. The living room opens to a covered terrace, which opens to a deck that leads to the pool and then to the beach. The custom rug conveys the impression of water. A. Rudin sofas; organic wood-stump coffee tables from Mexico City; light fixtures from Paul Ferrante.

ABOVE: Embroidered pillows and satin bedding collaborate beautifully with a leather nightstand artfully studded with nailheads. Nightstand custom made in Torreon, Mexico. RIGHT: A work of art by Mr. Brainwash is a surefire way to add unexpected modern fun and edge to an otherwise neutral resort bathroom. Contemporary light fixture from David Sutherland.

This guest bedroom was inspired by other exotic destinations. Customized headboards evoke a popular Moroccan motif. Chests inlaid with mother-of-pearl are Syrian. Hand-knotted rug is tribal Afghan.

An infinity pool entrance dead-ends at a bright yellow pot from Guadalajara and a towering saguaro cactus original to the property.

This private fire pit environment overlooking the desert is compensation for whoever inhabits the one guest room with no ocean view!

Under a traditional *latillo* roof, an intertwining infinity-style sculpture of whitewashed roots animates a fire-pit vignette. The swimming pool, which winds its way around the home, is more like a water feature or a meandering stream.

ARTISANAL
CONTEMPORARY

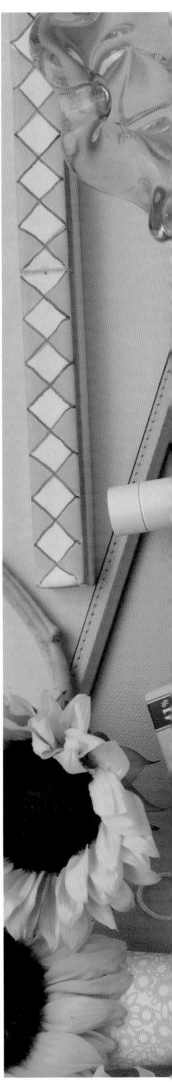

The silver lining of my nomadic childhood was the opportunity to experience firsthand the cultures and lifestyles of the Caribbean and Latin American countries I was obligated to call home. To a diligent student like myself, the differences between the street art of, say, Mexico City and the coastal art of Cartagena and Lima were mesmerizing. I paid attention to everything from museum collections to regional folkways, the Mestizo Baroque architecture of Bolivia to *los tres grandes* muralists of Mexico. By the time I arrived at design school, I was fluent in the artistic and artisanal traditions of a widely diverse set of cultures, ethnicities, and tribes.

No matter where I am, I always seek out the regional arts scene for authentic artifacts to incorporate into my work. It's not superficial tokenism; I really love to study and research indigenous building materials, design motifs, and native art. Mexican artisanal traditions

have long been integral to how I conceive resort home environments in Baja: the punched tin of San Miguel de Allende might find expression as a headboard for a guest room bed, or the carved hardwoods of Quintana Roo might be used for a built-in console or magnificent wall screen. I constantly use local stonework as both a paving material and a base for tables. I also like to highlight the artistic treatments of stone in carvings for outdoor tabletops and as focal pieces in gardens and poolscapes. If there's an evolved local tradition of ironwork, glassblowing, or tile making, then I'll commission bannisters, sconces, and fountains.

Tile work is an artisanal specialty all over Mexico, and I always look for ways to devote the most uniquely painted tiles as stair risers, wall art, pool accents, or mosaic murals. And textile traditions are a no-brainer for seamlessly weaving together other elements in a

room. Whether it's colorful Mexican embroidery or simple hand-dyed cotton, the colors and textures are beautifully suited to the resort climate—for a comfortable sofa, a festive draping under a thatched *palapa,* or a conversational grouping on a terrace.

There are favorite schemes that I tend to rely on but usually with a regional twist. For example, I like to use of Yucatan hardwood to install chevron parquet, or a slab of Mexican cocobolo burl wood to pair with a Lucite base for a floating modern table. This mix is both fun and site responsive, intersecting the familiar with the exotic. Local artisanal wares reliably add an earthy punctuation, so discovering a new generation of adventurous craftsmen creating exquisite, avant-garde work has been a thrill. If I'm being perfectly honest, my enthusiasm for the vibrant contemporary art and artisanal marketplace has lately provided me with a fairly distinctive design signature.

Incorporating the new breed of craftsman, artisan, and fine artist on the ground has proved inspirational and indispensable. Though they employ time-honored techniques, they're putting their own spin on long-standing disciplines and art forms, creating innovative and *nuevo* silhouettes in wrought ironwork, glazed tile, mosaic, pottery, textiles, basketwork, and furniture.

If one theme connects my recent interior design, it would be the celebration and promotion of vibrant contemporary paintings, large-scale sculpture, and experimental potteryscapes. I love to champion regional artists and artisans because, to me, their work amplifies the exotic atmosphere of the resort residence in Mexico. Escape is as much visceral and tactile as it is intellectual and social. It's my firm belief that regional specificity and reinvented tradition are really at the core of that experience.

LEFT: An Afghan runner lays the groundwork for a penthouse hallway. Abstract art hangs above an Ebanista console adorned with vintage *santos* and bright taxicab yellow urns from Guanajuato. ABOVE: A media room in muted spice tones accommodates multitudes with a wraparound sofa and huge custom ottomans. It's almost impossible to find a hand-knotted Moroccan rug this large. Almost.

LEFT: This unique interior space reflects multidimensional sophistication: chic silhouettes, luxe materials, natural elements, and impeccable artisanal craftsmanship. Massive handcrafted iron chandeliers echo the grandeur of both a vaulted ceiling constructed entirely with reclaimed beams and a soaring *bóveda* ceiling that is eight meters high. J. Robert Scott sofas. Lounge chairs from Mimi London.

This spectacular room expresses the provocative allure of contemporary artisanal style. For a client with renegade inclinations, I commissioned renowned ceramicist Peter Lane to create a wall treatment with an updated brutalist aesthetic. Elsewhere, clean horizontal lines merge with vintage luxury to create a singular interior that not only invites but amazes!

A curving wall became the perfect gallery for a collection of richly colored art glass pieces. A sculptural chair with an organic personality is stationed mid-hallway to push the whimsical attitude. At right, ornately painted, jewel-like Talavera tiles line the risers of a Cabo resort home staircase.

For the guest room of a Baja resort home, I employed a custom leather headboard, heavy wrought iron lamps, and bold ikat fabric to keep the mood dark and masculine. Artwork by renowned Mexican artist Pedro Friedeberg. Handmade Moroccan rug.

A home office/music room—Mexican resort-style—is made warm and texturally rich with Venetian plaster walls, dark woods, and earth tones. For a touch of whimsy, I found the Pancho Villa painting in San Miguel de Allende. Guitars from the owner's collection. RIGHT: Personality meets polish with a mishmash of printed linen pillows.

Folk art Dia de los Muertos (Day of the Dead) skeleton heads and tree of life candelabras can be found at open-air markets throughout Mexico. Images of the *calavera* Catrina, or elegant skull, are a ubiquitous symbol of the joyous holiday.

A view to drink for. Sometimes it's best to let nature do the work for you. This custom bar was designed to overlook the ravishing Sea of Cortez. Chairs by A. Rudin. Pendant lights from John Pomp.

ABOVE: Famed Mexican artist Victor Cauduro was commissioned to paint a favorite Baja vista on three slabs of stone. Custom-made curved sofas. Ceiling lights by Paul Ferrante. Sofa fabric by Robert Allen.

ABOVE RIGHT: *Papel picado* is a traditional Mexican folk art used throughout Mexico on Day of the Dead altars and streets during secular and religious celebrations. BELOW RIGHT: The historic downtown of San Juan del Cabo has a charming, relaxed, almost old-fashioned pace.

LEFT: An ocean-facing guest bedroom with a transitional feel and a nude palette gets a pop of color with a vintage French print.
RIGHT: A powder room shimmers with mirror, stone, and ceramic tiles. BELOW: A basement space is a high-functioning game room with a contemporary pool table. Rug by Aga John. Tiles by Ann Sacks.

A light-flooded master bedroom welcomes with natural finishes and a neutral palette of creams and browns accented with pops of teal.

Sleek and modern, this stunning resort living room was designed for entertaining and relaxation. In the foreground, a chic midcentury Venetian glass "Sputnik" chandelier adds pizzazz. Custom sofas are arranged around a coffee table fashioned from a slab of wood set on an acrylic base. Blue tone-on-tone cowfur rug by Kyle Bunting.

Built-in bunk beds provide plenty of space for visiting family and friends. Each bunk is decked out with an iPad holder, a reading light, and a coverlet of bold geometric fabric by Robert Allen.

This resort kitchen has all the artisanal components of an older Mexican estate but with up-to-date modern appliances and conveniences. Everything is custom-made: the hand-carved wood cabinetry, the Talavera tiles, the marble-topped islands, and the ceiling lamps.

ABOVE LEFT: A modernized *palapa* provides shade and shelter for an outdoor dining room. BELOW LEFT: As stylish as it is functional, this marble-topped island anchors the kitchen, while blond wood cabinetry keeps the space sleek and sophisticated. ABOVE: A luscious brown and white color story creates a warm and cozy guest room.

This gorgeous living room overlooking the Sea of Cortez is both casual and elegant and conveys a Zen-like tranquility. Pillows are fashioned with Fortuny fabric and Robert Allen trim. Upholstered coffee table from Guadalajara. Rug custom made in Nepal. Ceiling light of hand-blown crystal globes by John Pomp.

The view here is the showstopper. From this vantage point, you can see the mountains, the desert and the oceans. Outdoor furniture by Thomas Lavin. Rotating daybed by Dedon.

THE OUTDOOR OASIS

Most resorts are situated in extraordinary physical locations. Whether alpine lodges, desert retreats or island hideaways, nature delivers the knockout venue and sets the stage for a magnificent escape. For the last few years, my particular niche has been a stretch of geography along the Pacific Ocean that is both dramatically rocky and seductively sandy. The essence of a resort home along the Mexican coastline is its proximity to picturesque mountains meeting the sea, and earth-toned desert meeting lush blue water. My job is to enhance these natural attractions without obscuring them, which is an essential yet subtle art; after all, even the freshest fish taco benefits from some squeezed lime! I design with an indoor/ outdoor template in mind, facilitating the movement of residents from sun to shade to sun again, like meandering onshore breezes.

Outdoor rooms, such as freestanding *palapas*, are specialized with regional architectural features and sculptural arrangements of cactus, agave and palms. Resort homes in Mexico tend towards an abundance of seating options decked out in a colorful riot of cushions, which are as luxuriously indispensable as the outdoor kitchen and built-in grill. The sights and sounds of the ocean are echoed in scalloped conversational nooks, splashing fountains and iridescent tile work. I personally prefer rattan for alfresco spaces, but I can go all out with elegant and unexpected furniture in these transitional areas, creating indistinct moments between indoors and out. Beyond the loggia threshold I like to design a cozy but more exposed terrace with outdoor rugs and swagged fabric hung between carved stone columns. Oversized and outlandish wicker

furniture, bright umbrellas and always more, more, more cushions create gathering spots for sun worshippers and post-swim bathers who want to air-dry in plush comfort.

Beyond the home, a broad expanse of lawn will typically surround a pool, perhaps with an infinity design whose lines merge with the sky and sea. Loungers, umbrellas, glazed ceramic planters and built-in features complete the scene. The coup de grace, for me, is a stunning lighting scheme designed to highlight distinctive landscape features from dusk till dawn and transform the space into an exotic and captivating nighttime environment. This is how whim and wherewithal conspire to lead host and guest far into sublime oblivion at his or her own pace.

At the heart of my design philosophy is the belief that leisure time is the greatest luxury of all in our otherwise fast-paced digital world, and that the real value in escaping to a resort is to disregard time altogether in favor of personal restoration and communal recreation. Who doesn't love taking a nap during an afternoon rainburst in the desert, or watching the sun dip below a liquid horizon, or splashing around in the salty clean tangle of seaweed at the beach? I just want my clients to take full advantage of these increasingly rare experiences. I want their homes to be used thoroughly in ever-evolving sequences. And I want every evening to end with a transcendent sunset or late-night swim or fireside tête-à-tête. I love the decorative arts, but I'm also mindful of when and how to let nature do the work for me.

For outdoor environments in Baja, I always love to unite the traditional with the contemporary, and the vintage with the new. ABOVE: I utilize wrought iron chandeliers and chairs with a hand carved cantera stone coffee table. RIGHT: I outfitted terrace benches with built-in handmade "arm" side tables for a surreal touch of whimsy.

Under a *latillo* roof, a private terrace is as restful and relaxed as the French bulldog's guest bedroom. The wall niche was the perfect spot for this rare, vintage vessel from Oaxaca.

Fire pits not only add visual appeal but they also become a natural gathering spot, especially on chilly nights along the coast. An outdoor bar area feels like an actual room in an enclosed sunken space. ABOVE: A bridge over a wraparound pool leads to a conversation pit with built-in seating, an array of pillows, and a chic fire bowl.

This traditional courtyard with cantera stone arches reflects the gracious architecture of traditional Mexico. At once intimate and grand, ample seating amid colorful pillows makes this outdoor living room stylish and entertainment friendly. The location offers stunning views of the ocean and mountains beyond. Vintage pots from Guadalajara

With an unobstructed view of a white sandy beach and shimmering sapphire water, the dining area brings sleek style and a chic neutral palette to an airy Cabo resort home. Cool Crema Marfil floors make a classically elegant design statement, while the John Pomp ceiling light and Holly Hunt chairs keep the contemporary ball bouncing.

Polished wrought iron furniture from Formations and swagged outdoor curtain fabric by Robert Allen create a stately atmosphere for this breathtaking terrace overlooking lush grounds and a shimmering swimming pool.

Teak furniture from David Sutherland and a vintage table from Morocco occupy the terrace of a Cabo San Lucas penthouse. The rooftop getaway offers a lap pool, Jacuzzi, and stunning views of the Pacific Ocean.

On an upstairs balcony overlooking the Sea of Cortez, custom hanging daybeds dripping with a blend of luscious pillows in sublime patterns suggest the essence of barefoot luxury.

A sunken conversation fire pit is built right into the pool of this intoxicating Baja resort home. Accessible by floating stones, this feature adds a sense of drama and glamour. Outdoor fabric by Le Jardin. Jorge Marin sculpture.

An outdoor fireplace warms this small penthouse terrace furnished with hanging daybed, custom tie-dyed pillows, and traditional Mexican star lights.

Hanging daybeds by Dedon float over the shallow part of a swimming pool. Mounted side tables mean you can climb aboard with a drink and not leave for a while. Locally sourced simply styled pots hold desert-friendly cactuses and succulents.

The star of this outdoor dining and living room is the vein cut travertine floor. A handcrafted Mexican iron chandelier presides over the penthouse terrace.

Rear view of a gorgeous Cabo estate that is the epitome of relaxed, luxury living. The home is equipped with a retractable outdoor fabric roof that can turn a covered balcony into an open-air space.

An open, gracious space combines kitchen and living room right on the beach. The curved counter echoes the custom rounded sofa and swooping standing floor lamps from Armani Home. An old piece of wood mounted on iron becomes a striking sculpture.

This columned terrace includes faux stone chairs, a real stone table, and tiled flooring that simulates a carpet. The wrought iron ceiling light was sourced locally. Indoor/outdoor fabric by Gaiti. ABOVE: Thatched huts on Playa Palmilla. BELOW: Illuminated umbrellas cast an enchanting glow poolside.

A simple upstairs terrace off a guest bedroom is furnished with an Indonesian bench and chairs upholstered in a Perennials outdoor fabric.

A mid-pool sunken conversation pit, pillowed and warmed by fire, overlooks the glittering lights of San Jose del Cabo as night falls.

An outdoor room with a view. The pool and terrace serve as focal points of a sprawling Cabo retreat. Covered terraces, fire pit, Jacuzzi, outdoor bar, dining room, and grill deliver every component essential for complete and utter blissful relaxation, barefoot-luxury style.

ACKNOWLEDGMENTS

Being in the business of creativity on demand is a team effort. I could not make *interior beauty* happen without my amazing and tireless design team, who support me and help execute my wild ideas. Thank you, to all of the incredible people who live and breathe interior design with me:

The Bean—office mascot

Ana Paula Gastelum—Interior Architect

Carolina Castrejon—Sr. Designer

Enriqueta Guzman—Sr. Designer

Brianne Buyarski—Sr. Designer

Ivanna Bross—Designer

Paola Castillo—Designer

Ana Mal Vaez—Design Assistant

Patty Santos—Office Manager

Karelina Olivarez—Purchasing Manager

Jessica Reyes—Purchasing Assistant

Hortencia Zamudio—Personal Assistant

Adrian Estrada—Installation Manager

Manuel Jurado—Installations

And a special thank-you to all of the people who helped create this book. Without you, getting the ideas out of my head and making them reality would not have happened.

Madge Baird—for believing in me once again and guiding me through this process.

Mel B—for your words. All of them.

Virginia Snow & Sheryl Dickert—for the beautiful graphic work and book design.

Hector Velasco Fazio—for all of your amazing photographs and friendship.

Sabina Todd—for always being there.

But most of all, the only reason this book exists is because of the amazing clients who have trusted me throughout the years and have given me opportunity to work in their homes and help execute their dreams. The photos in this book are windows into their lives and my memories working with them.

John & Michelle Keller

Travis & Mike Farncombe

Jim & Laura Hirschmann

Doug Heltne

Richard & Betti Robinson

Bill & Jan Sanger

Murray & Gaye Farncombe

Jorge & Lupita Zepeda

Steve & Leticia Trauber

Matt & Lindsey Farncombe

Bob & Taffi Saltzmann

Scott & Marylin Durham

Kenny & Laurie Goodman

Joe & Suzanne Sutton

Bill & Sako Fisher

Tom & Beth Moore

John & Leticia Hahn

Published by
Gibbs Smith
P.O. Box 667
Layton, Utah 84041

1.800.835.4993 orders
www.gibbs-smith.com

Printed and bound in China
18 19 20 21 22   5 4 3 2 1

Gibbs Smith books are printed on either recycled, 100% post-consumer
waste, FSC-certified papers or on paper produced from sustainable PEFC-
certified forest/controlled wood source. Learn more at www.pefc.org.

Library of Congress Control Number: 2017952201
ISBN: 978-1-4236-4937-3